AF435173

COLEEN LIESTOCK

*my sorrow
drowned
the stars*

my sorrow drowned
the stars

disclaimer

This collection covers mental health topics such as anxiety, suicidal thoughts, and other subjects that may touch the sensibilities of certain people.
Take care of yourself.

© Coleen Liestock, 2025
Cover made on © Canva
ISBN 979-10-977115-0-4
Legal deposit: June 2025

The Intellectual Property Code prohibits copies or reproductions intended for collective use. Any representation or reproduction, in whole or in part, made by any means whatsoever, without the consent of the author or his successors, is unlawful and constitutes an infringement under articles L.335-2 et seq. of the French Intellectual Property Code.

*to the 'four years ago' me
who would never have thought
to still be here
to write these lines*

summary

preface

this book is not about love
or just a little

it tells you
you came
you lived
you will live on
and on

it does not talk about
disappointed feelings
or only a few times

it sometimes speaks
        of those tears in the sheets
full of pain
of shame
of sorrow
        those crystal tears
from
our rivers of thoughts
which grow
some flower fields
already wilted
of too great a despair
but also young sprouts
carriers of "maybe"
and trembling audacity

this book tells you
that you are your Sun
your Moon
your entire universe
and that to cherish
your stars of emotions
your heart of gold
and your infinite soul
no one is better placed
than your own person

I. DISSOLUTION

when I met you
I thought
that you would give me
everything I needed

I didn't know
that you would take it all
even
what I didn't have

I saw you
knew you
wanted you

had you

cried for you
cuddled you
hated you

I put
my head under water
to drown myself
in the same sea as you
        if we're going to die
        we might as well
        do it together
your grief
became mine

I wanted to go up
        I could not find
        any ground to push off from
I lost
your hand on the way
        and my soul with it
I forgot
what breathing felt like
I let myself
be lured by the abyss
feeding the dark envy
of getting lost in it

and in the hope
that it engulfed you too
        if we're going to die
        we might as well
        do it together

because you don't deserve
to survive
when a gaping hole
fills my chest
with bitter blood
and scarlet memories

33.

it has been years
but
I haven't forgotten

I was the leaf
under the suitcase
you were dragging

striking the ground
again and again

breaking
bit by bit

abandoned on the floor
with no apology

watching you go away
the end of my stem
still holding
some dried-up remorses

you had the gift
of telling me
you loved me
while
showing me the opposite

what were words then
compared to
the unapologetic power
of your shameless actions

you blamed me
for abandoning you
but when we were two
I was already alone

I
fixed my heart
with a wire
cutting burning piercing
the shreds that remained

it's
a little better now

the one
who suffered the most
is my soul
bearer of memories
that I sometimes distort
to see you again
kind and loving
or
bitterly awful
        to punish myself
        for being too happy
        from time to time

my heart is in
a glass jar
barely palpitating
bloody as can be
it prays
to be released
from this vain embrace

I was an adult
in a relationship
of innocent children

one day
my arms broke
facing
this too heavy load
that you didn't
help me carry

I oscillate between
the impression
of not existing

and the even worse one
of being too visible

a beam
in the middle of the night
we didn't ask for
that burns our eyes
and that we regret
having looked at

I spent months
running
after your smile
so much
that I forgot mine

maybe I am
one of those people
for whom *I love you*
isn't so important anymore

or maybe
on the contrary
it's too precious to me

and so I repeat it
without reason
to dull its meaning
in my heart
in the naive hope
of not bleeding too much
the day I say it for real
and that only silence
comes as an answer

I pray
for you to look at me
when I cry
and ask yourself
if it's your fault

I wanted
to stop it all
because I didn't know
how to survive
in a world
that didn't want me

we are told
to promote difference
but not one
that bothers or disturbs too much

we try to walk
while everyone
pushes us
so we crawl
we are run over
we slouch our shoulders
we forget ourselves

nonetheless
there is always someone
to point the finger
and make us feel
lower than Earth
        as if it weren't
        already the case

before
everything was easy

when I had to pretend
put on a coat
a mask
and a smile

walk
right ahead
by dodging
and skipping
around hollows and bumps

now
the hollows are ravines
the bumps cliffs
the coat is in pieces
the mask carbonised
            from touching
            the fire in me

the smile
disappeared
buried
with other crumbs
of a me
I never really knew

the varnish of my face
peeled off
wore out

everyone is surprised
by what lies behind
            me the first

31

it is said that
the nightmares we dwell in
only appear
when the sun sets
and silence falls

then why
is my head full
as soon as morning comes?

why
        does my heart beat so fast
        does my belly tighten so
        even when the weather is nice
        even when it is daylight
        even when I don't know why
        even when I don't want to
        even when I'm told
        that it's okay
        ?

stopping myself from crying
made me feel
in control one thing
in my life
as did
drawing
red roses on my skin
not sleeping
for nights
smiling
to those I love
lying
without reason
dreaming
of a happiness beyond reach

it is easy
to lie
especially
with words

with gestures
it's harder
with the heart
it's impossible

except
if we've trained
like me
to bury everything
to put it all simply
in order to please

giving a name
to my emotions
seemed even harder
than experiencing them

I felt them swarming
in me
like animals in cages
that I sometimes let out
all teeth showing

I didn't know
their date of arrival
their duration of stay
their identity

they were there
I did not dare
make them go away
so
I suffered them
   I was dominated
   by unnamed
   and faceless monsters
   and when I tried
   to take over
   I always ended up
   more chained than before

if I could have chosen
between you
and my worst nightmare
I would have
dipped
both feet
in the dark
of my nights
> *when I do now*
> *it's you I discover*
> *at the turn*
> *of an unfinished dream*

it's not a shadow
that I hit

it's an abyss
that swallowed me whole

37

I am not unwell enough
to accept
the hands
I am being offered

I never felt at the top
but when you arrived
I felt myself slipping
down
down
to the bottom of an abandoned hill
                              39

and once
I hit the ground
I started digging
to join you
in the infernal kingdom
where you
have me as your queen
          a captive queen
          of desires
          not even her own

love is also that

folding in four
in ten
in thousands
saying yes
to everything
for everything
curling up
begging for forgiveness
no longer having a taste for anything
except him

love is
being in pain
because of the other
and believing
that it is normal
that we deserve it
because love is a fight
not just
a peaceful walk
so
we must take up arms
stab them in our heart
and give it all
at all costs
even if means
to lose ourselves

love is also that
        I thought

it's as if in me
everything was boiling
everything was swarming
everything was rumbling

and then
that I imploded
my feelings scattered on the ground
like waste
that I no longer wanted
> *I never*
> *wanted them*
> *I never*
> *understood*
> *why they were there*

and these crumbs
come together again
catch fire
go up in smoke
in broad daylight
their trail
in the sky
showing the extent
of my past sorrows

I liked to live
inside me
until
you invaded me
and my pretty house
became
a set of scorched
and haunted
ruins

there was a time
when I thought I could
taste
innocent happiness

I thought
that being with you
would make me better

I clung
to this thought
until I had
my palms covered in blood

I could not conceive
of reaching joy
without you

I imagined
a cottoned future
bearing
the taste of your eyes
and infinite

there was a time
where a mirage
shaped my reality
and where real life
faded from my head
        as if
        it wasn't worth
        being truly lived

I think
that my anger
engulfed me whole

it left nothing
if not
a viper's skin
torn during
this too-early moulting

I lean
on the void
look
down
and let myself fall
your arms
will not catch me
I know it

36.

falling in love
is madness
that we realise
only once we've lived it
          and that it has defeated us

and madness
is to believe
that we are strong enough to bandage
our own wounds
with denial
or hollow jokes

that's why

the craziest of all fools
is not the one
who makes the most laugh

but the one
who behind their pirouettes
hides
a heart in pieces
that they refuse
to have fixed
        out of fear
        to confront themselves
        to those emotions
        buried deep within
        and to admit they have lost out
                once again
        to their fervour

the craziest of all fools
loves unconditionally
        that is
        what drives their madness
they know they will suffer
and that they
will not be treated
        what good is it
        to still live
        if it is
        to suffer again?

it is said
that words
cure the ills

but in my case
it is rather the ache
on my skin
that soothe the words
you left there

I felt myself rotting
as if
I were a flower
      not very nice
      not very green
a flower of the desert

and that
you were the air
too moist
wet
too fresh
icy even
who had drowned me
had made me sick
made me
lose my leaves
and my reason

      I ended up
      in a trash can

I forged myself
in the burning flames
of my tears
as golden as my soul

before you stole it
you even
captured my cries
in your leather bag

my smiles glide
resonate
spark
and vanish
as crazy as if
a blaze were fizzling out
under/beneath
the weakness of a breeze

I could have done better
I could have confessed
what was wrong

but the words
did not come out
trapped by my fear
of displeasing you
and the anxiety
of a dispute
I would come out losing

I felt responsible
for what happened to me
I was
but just a little

because you too
could have done better
we are both
responsible
for our own misfortune

and if love
means suffering together
worse still
because of the other
I would rather
never see it again

you planted a seed
in me
with your words
your eyes
your hands
you cultivated it
      I would have preferred
      that you hadn't

it grew
and now
a rotten tree
gnawed
from leaves to roots
has settled

its branches twitch
around my belly
its buds hatch
and pour into me
the remnants
of your words
and its bark
is imprinted
with your whole persona

this tree
continues to grow
even if you're gone
the frozen memories
still feed it

I tried
time and again
to uproot it
with my bare hands
but it did me
even more harm

53

maybe this tree
cannot be removed
maybe you will
always be in me
maybe I don't want
to let you go
maybe I got used
to hurting because of you
and I no longer know
how to live
any other way
        in peace
        with
        what you did to me

what I did not know
before being with you

is that I was gold
that you reduced to lead

weighed down by your words
and new evils
I am now waiting
for a new alchemist
to come and make amends

II. PURIFICATION

I took a breath
pinched my nose
and plunged into myself

I did not know
what was hiding there
but I hoped
to uncover my secrets

69.
clowns
are always the saddest
I thought
that it was a lie
> how could
> a clown cry?
I know now
how wrong I was
when the make-up
on my own skin
erased
my misfortunes
> *at least until the evening*
and served as my armour
I understood
that the clown
> blind
> to his own life
had been me
all along

if you believe
that I think about you
when I fall asleep
when I get up
when I'm alone
when I'm happy
when I'm drunk
when I eat
when I walk
when I see a couple in the street
when I dream of later
when I think of before
when I feel the now

you're right

leaving you
was
the easiest
and the hardest
decision
of my life

how
can you walk away
from someone
you thought you cherished
for years
someone
who destroyed you as much
as they taught you life?

I never understood
how people could
think so much good
about me

it was wrong
too delicious
to be sincere

so I ran away
leaving behind
a disappointed heart
to protect mine
already too damaged
behind its paper wall

I do not feel
legitimate
asking for help
when I'm the one
who is the problem

one might think
that once we know
we're not well
we're already halfway there

I don't believe it

I knew
that I wasn't okay
and yet I felt
even more lost than before

how was I supposed
to get out
of the mess
I had dived into
of my own free will?

I just wish
that someone would
hold my hand
tell me it will be fine
and believe it for me

when he rejected me
I told myself
that it was normal
logical
that I deserved it
because nobody
          no one
would ever be able
to love me
for who I am
          even
          wearing
          a mask of steel
          I doubt
          I'll ever
          attract anyone

the fatigue
weighs on me
the recovery
eludes me
how
can one live
when nothing
has the taste
one would like to give it?

draped in impure silk
I move towards the void
of immaculate black
outstretching its large arms
that await me

my hesitation
evaporates in a breath
the fear of my fate
disappears as I leap

how can we know
we are feeling better
when around us
everything seems to be
a tangle
of knots
dipped in petrol
with burnt ends
and tangled threads?

I rowed
with both arms
in a stormy sea

I kept
staring at
a distant island
on the horizon

then
it disappeared
just like that

I found myself
drifting alone

I shouted
a dolphin came through
he smiled at me
but it was not enough

    my boat capsized

nobody can love me
if I don't do anything
to deserve it

99.1

I keep taking refuge
with those
whom I know
will not cherish me

to regain
the familiar feeling
that I had
by your side

and I try
with all my might
to prove to them
why they should change their minds
while reassuring myself
persuading myself
that I cannot be loved
and that they are right
not to pay me any attention
          just like
          you did

99.2

so when
once
I bumped into someone
nearly nice
who whispered to me
that I was pretty
interesting
          interesting
remarkable
brilliant
          more so than a night star
I turned around
and ran towards
a warm chasm
where I could
dive into my tears
and flood myself with hatred

give me back the time
I spent
pretending to love you

if I could go back in time
I would like
to talk to myself before I met you

to tell me how
I am now
what you changed me into
how you pulverised me
bombed me
consumed me

I would say to the old me
to stay away from you
not to talk to you

        I'm not sure
        that I would listen

I stayed
because I did not have
anywhere else
to go

all that time I thought
that an accompanied hell
was more enjoyable
than a lonely grief

once you were no longer there
everything was much better
I breathed again
my mind brightened

I admit it
I saw
the light
at the end of the tunnel

but a shadow
          mine
ruined this picture
because
I realised
that the problem
came not only from you
        my pain
        came not only from you

I was quite capable
of destroying myself on my own
all you did
was push me harder

I put you behind me
eject you from my heart
with a fanfare of tears
        you never
        really existed there
        anyway

I tell myself
that everything will be fine
now that I have regained
my beloved solitude

but learning
to adore me again
is much harder
than I thought it would be

everything is mixed up
last week
was only yesterday
and thinking about tomorrow
makes my heart choke

I don't know
anything about today
I don't know
how to get back to life

I don't know
how to find myself again
around a corner
that I don't remember
ever turning

I wander
in search of a glow
that would cleanse me
of a
well deserved guilt

I'm looking out
for a more flowery morning
an endless night
the easiest route
to flee from my future

I felt myself
relive
breathe
as if
a new me had been born

or
that you had buried it
and that
it had come back

I understood
that you were not good for me
when it was too late
when you
had already hurt me
wrinkled me
crushed me

but I also believe
it is never too late

I don't know
if I can
be repaired

but I managed
to escape from you
before I was
completely
reduced to ashes

I guess
then
that it wasn't too late

I was no longer afraid

suddenly
life was simple
easy
like a ride at sea
a yoghurt cake
a laugh in the night

in the middle
of this oil spill
a flower grew
out of nowhere
bearer of strange hopes
of feeling better one morning

my mind settles
my heart breathes
calm
finally

and then I think of you

III. FUSION

the sun's rays
on my wounded skin
remind me of
a vivid misfortune
and urge me to cherish
a bliss
I thought impossible
it was hiding
in little moments

I then ignored
how to seize it

but I learned
how to reach out
and harvest
the flowers within my grasp
and even
to raise my heels
and catch
the ripest fruits
of the sunny orchard

I do not have
the monopoly
on pain
but I have the right
to scream
that I'm hurting

I was there for you
but who was there for me?

when the pain was too strong
when the desire to fly outweighed the will to fight
when I was no longer enough and my soul got stained
when the empty room swallowed me dead and spat me out
alive
when I no longer existed
not even in my dreams

who was there
when my throat was on fire
inhabited by fierce devils
when it was filled
with scrawny weeping
and where
despite myself
grew all my anguishes

when I dared not say anything
for fear
my demons would escape
and contaminate the world
when pretending to be fine
hurt less
than admitting my pain

who was there
for me?

the hardest part of all
was knowing
that there were people
ready to help me
            to walk
and that I did not
            welcome them

one must be brave
to ask for help
and at the time
I wasn't

I didn't dare show
how my heart was breaking
how many fights I led
as my fears devoured me
how deep I was sinking

I thought
that it would make me weak
but what destroyed me
was keeping it all inside
because I ended up
imploding

healing from you
is my hardest fight

I was always told
that I was different
I never knew
if it was flattery
or criticism

some whispered it to me
as a secret
I had to keep
and not disclose

or one shouted it to me
like an anthem
that I'd have
to cherish on my own

some would sigh
with a dose
of fatigue
and misunderstanding

"you are too different"
they said
without noticing
that I understood it
just by how
they looked at me

I am different
but I'm not just that
so I'm waiting
to discover the rest

I found the light again
but your shadow still hovers
above me

thinking about you
for just a moment
makes me want
to sink
forever

I suffered so much
with you
that I'm afraid
to run away
from every person
who could bring me
something good
for fear of spoiling it
by thinking
that it's too good
to be true

you didn't notice
anything
that is why
I can't bring myself
to hate you
as much as I would like

after
the darkness
I knew
I had trouble seeing
the light
where it already was
      actually
      it had always been there
      I just wasn't able
      to distinguish it

I feel myself
reborn
little by little
away from you
I'm not better
not worse
I'm just
different

a part of me
does not know calm
so it creates within me
a new void
that feeds
the monster of anxiety
glad to have
a piece of me
to chew on still

if you didn't like me
it's that I wasn't good enough

I never told myself
that you didn't love me enough
simply because
you didn't *see* me enough
      that you bathed me
      in a smokescreen
      of the one
      you really wanted

actually
I never knew why
you gave me such a feeling
of being unloved
I think
that it was the case
but you showed it badly
and what I should have known
is that
it was not
my fault
never
my fault

to be in love
is not to love the other
it is to love who we are with them

I have doubted
my worth
so much
that I have come
to ask myself
if I was really worth
something

I know
that some
have done a lot
for me

I still ask too much
and don't know
how to satisfy myself
with an ocean of love
      I don't know what to do with
      that floods me
      and leaves me thirsty still

93.

I am

a clown
whose raft
has broken
several times

a fool
who has drowned
in the ocean
of their emotions

a princess
fallen from
a cardboard
pedestal

a soul in pain
that the void
and night
have embraced

but I am also

the queen
of my own kingdom

the captain
of my enchanted ship

and nothing
can dethrone me
can prevent me
from realising myself
from becoming
the one I wish
to be now

I aspire
only to complete
the oh-so-complex puzzle
of my life
all the pieces
will come
I simply have
to wait for them
in peace

I dream
of the best
because truly
that is
what I deserve

I don't know
if what I do
is right or wrong
I'm just trying
to do my best

when I saw
what
you had turned me into
I felt stupid

I didn't know
how to love myself anymore

it took me time
to manage
to take
a step forward

to look at myself
in a mirror
without seeing
your reflection next to mine

sometimes
I still feel
your hands on me

other days
I forget
that you even exist

I know
you will remain
etched into me
for years to come
forever perhaps

but I'm working
on the pain
it causes me
surely it will
fade with time
because I refuse
to let it devour me
more than
it already has

change
is scary
terrifying
even more so
than a monster under the bed

so
I ran away
until
I no longer had a choice
but to confront it

once this was done
I was in pain
and at the same time
a strange gleam
of sweetness
invited itself
into the void
left between two fears

it is said that
the one who is left behind
suffers more
than the one who leaves

but it takes courage
to choose
to put an end
to a relationship with no direction or purpose
one that consumes us
more than it nourishes us

one must be prepared
to let their heart bleed
in the face of a decision
for which they are
solely responsible

one must be prepared
to see the other cry

one must be prepared
not to flinch
to preserve
their own happiness
even at the expense
of the other's
for once
in their life

I am gradually learning
that others are
not all like you
that I deserve
love and respect
just as much as anyone

I find it strange
to have someone
who takes
care of me
without expecting anything
in return

66.

it's been years
I haven't forgotten
that it was your fault

I will never forgive you
but I put my energy
into loving myself
rather
than hating you

I dream of romance
a delicate novel
filled with sorrow

but to love another
I must
cherish myself first
because it would be absurd
to imagine
again
that a being other than me
could offer me
the happiness
I keep chasing
without ever catching it

my anguish kills me
faster than a cigarette
lurking deep
in the recesses of my chest
it ate my heart
and though I
relish the pain
        as if it were
        what I deserved
I refuse to let it
annihilate me
because I chose
that one day
it would become
my best friend

happiness is strange

it flies with
the candour of a child
on a swing

it rings
sweeter than a
"come back
you'll catch a cold"

it tastes
even better
than Sunday pie

it doesn't show
doesn't make a sound
but I know it's there
near me

it goes away
sometimes

I let it slip away
no more chasing it
knowing it will return
when it feels like it

happiness is strange
strangely perfect

an unknown
mixes in an enchanted bowl

three drops of assurance
two doses of uncertainty
twelve pounds of pain
just as much grief
twice as much joy

everything clashes
ignites
a fiery cloud
escapes from the beaker

and comes to life before my eyes
a future
I no longer dreamed of

I know
that it won't get better
right away
not today
not tomorrow

I just believe
in a better day
soon

I cling to it
firmly
without burning my hands
gently
without weakening either

the chemistry
of my life
has not finished
reacting

I'll never return
to the golden state
        because I got
        too worn out
        too damaged

but I know
that these cracks
have made me more beautiful
they remind me
that I have lived
that I am alive
that I will live on
and on

thank you.

notes

DISSOLUTION

the Work in black
ruled by Saturn
aims
to calcine
the base metal
pierce it raw
and let it surrender
to the release
of its darkest secrets

PURIFICATION

the Work in white
blessed by the Moon
lets the broken stone's
consciousness expand
it who firmly believes
in being reborn one morning
and marveling
at the newness
of its existence

notes

FUSION

the Work in red
governed by the Sun
transmutes for good
the rock into aether
through flames and hope
spirit and matter
reconcile
in intimate fullness
shaded in grey

ALCHEMY

alchemy grants the wish
of ordinary mercury
to transmute into gold
through the divine union
of essence and substance
ataraxia is reached
through full suffering
welcomed by the body

acknowledgements

strangely, those few words are the most difficult to extract from my mind.

thank you Margot, Zoe, my first readers.

thanks to myself because if I have learned anything from writing this book, it is that we should be grateful to ourselves first.

thanks to you, holding this book between your fingers.

thank you for existing.

xoxo,
coco

author's note

If you liked this collection, you can message me on Instagram, leave a review on Amazon or on reading platforms like Booknode and Goodreads.

You can also talk about this book around you, recommend it to your loved ones – because word of mouth is even more valuable for us self-published authors.

Thank you again for reading, and I invite you to join me on Instagram to be aware of my next releases!

The collection's playlist is available on Spotify:

Instagram : coleen_liestock

Legal deposit : June 2025